FAMILY
Life
ISSUES

Growing as a
Single Parent

By Janet Robson

D0877724

CPH™
SAINT LOUIS

Editor: Rodney L. Rathmann
Editoral Assistant: Phoebe W. Wellman

Write to Library for the Blind, 1333 S. Kirkwood Road, St. Louis, MO 63122-7295 to obtain *Growing as a Single Parent* in braille or large print for the visually impaired.

Contents

Introduction

▲ How to Use This Course

This course has been especially prepared for use in small group settings. It may, however, also be used as a self study or in a traditional Sunday morning Bible class.

▲ Planning for a Small Group Study

1. *Select a leader* for the course or a leader for the day. It will be the leader's responsibility to secure needed materials, to keep the discussion moving, and to help involve everyone.

2. *Emphasize sharing.* Your class will work best if the participants feel comfortable with one another and if all feel that their contributions to the class discussion are important and useful. Take the necessary time at the beginning of the course to get to know one another. You might share names, occupations, hobbies, etc. Share what you expect to gain from this course.

Invite participants to bring photos of their families to the first session to pass around as they introduce themselves and tell about the individual members of their families. Be open and accepting. Don't force anyone to speak. The course will be most helpful if participants willingly share deep feelings, problems, doubts, fears, and joys. That will require building an atmosphere of openness, trust, and caring between one another. Take time to build relationships among participants. That time will not be wasted.

3. Help participants apply the concepts included in each session. After each week's study, suggested activities are

included. An old Chinese proverb summarizes the "why?" of the activities:

I hear and I forget;
I see and I remember;
I do and I understand.

The purpose of the activities is to help participants do and thus understand. Encourage everyone to take time to do one or more of them.

4. Encourage participants to invite their friends—including their unchurched friends—to be a part of this study.

▲ As You Plan to Lead the Group

1. Read this guide in its entirety before you lead the first session.

2. Use the Leaders Notes found in the back of this guide.

3. Pray each day for those who join the group.

4. As you prepare for each session, study the Bible texts thoroughly. Work through the exercises for yourself. Depend on the Holy Spirit. Expect His presence; He will guide you and cause you to grow. God will not let His Word return empty (Isaiah 55:11) as you study it both individually and with the others in the group.

5. Do not expect the Spirit to do your work for you. Start early. Prepare well. As time permits, do additional reading about the topic.

6. Begin and end with prayer.

7. Begin and end on time. Punctuality is a courtesy to everyone and can be a factor that will encourage discussion.

8. Find ways to keep the session informal: Meet in casual surroundings. Arrange seating so participants can face one another. Ask volunteers to provide refreshments.

9. Keep the class moving. Limit your discussion to questions of interest to the participants. Be selective. You don't need to cover every question and every Bible verse.

10. Try to build one another up through your fellowship and study. You have your needs; other group members have theirs. Together you have a lot to gain.

11. Be sensitive to any participants who may have needs

related to the specific problems discussed in this course, especially anyone who may need Christian counseling and professional help.

12. Be a "gatekeeper." That means you may need to shut the gate on one person while you open it for someone else. Try to involve everyone, especially those who hesitate to speak.

▲ If You Are Using This Study on Your Own

1. Each time you sit down to study a session, ask the Holy Spirit for guidance and counsel. Expect Him to work through His Word to encourage, motivate, and empower you to grow in your faith.

2. Study the Bible texts, printed in the course, with special care. God works through His Word. In it you will find power. Read each text slowly, several times.

3. Write answers in the spaces provided. Avoid the temptation just to "think" your responses. Writing will force you to be specific. It's in that specificity you are most likely to identify crucial issues for yourself. Check the Leaders Notes in the back of this guide for information you may find helpful as you go along.

4. Pray as you work. Ask God to show you what He wants you to see about Him, about yourself, and about your family situation.

Meeting My Needs **1** ▼

Opening Prayer

Heavenly Father, we thank and praise You and for the life You have given us. Today as we open our hearts to Your Word, help us to rededicate ourselves and our families to You. Comfort us with the forgiveness You have made available to us through Your Son, Jesus Christ. Empower us by Your love and guide us by the power of Your Holy Spirit as we begin this study. In Jesus' name we pray. Amen.

Focusing Our Attention

Share with the group which of the following movie titles reminds you of your life with your children this past week and why.

_____Terms of Endearment

_____I Want to Live

_____One Flew Over the Cuckoo's Nest

_____Ordinary People

_____All Quiet on the Western Front

_____The Miracle Worker

_____The Best Years of Our Lives

Going It Alone

God has given parents, including those who are parenting alone, others in the Christian community to listen, understand, encourage, and help. Because God loves us, we can love and care for others, even as we face the struggles and challenges of our own daily lives. Listen now to Ellen as she shares about her life.

When my husband left, it was difficult at first. Then after I got my real-estate license, I was able to support myself and my two teenage daughters. Gradually, with God's help the girls were able to put most of their anger behind them and began adjusting to their new lifestyle. Since the beginning of our new life together we have shared many positive events. Lately we are closer than we have ever been before.

Work with a partner or in small groups to list the ways parenting as a single parent compares to parenting in a two-parent household.

Similar   **Different**

What's Happening to Me?

Ellen was able to list a number of positive events that had occurred in her daughters' lives. "You know," she confided, "I feel so responsible for their happiness." Then she added with a sigh, "It doesn't seem to matter whether I'm happy."

Ellen expresses a theme common to parents and especially single parents: She has lost herself in the goal of meeting the needs of her children. Perhaps she would even have trouble identifying what her own needs are.

With a partner or in a group of three or four, read the following comments made by single parents. Listen for the specific needs expressed by each. In the space provided, write the need you hear expressed in each quote.

1. "If I could tell people one thing," says Kate, a divorced mother of three young children, "It would be, 'Don't judge me—I'm my own worst critic.' "

2. "It's so hard for me to ever be alone. Getting a baby-sitter just so I can do something I really want to do by myself is out of the question."

3. "I only get to see my kids on weekends, and the rest of the week I haven't a clue what they're doing. They tell me about school and about their friends, but I still feel like an outsider. Sometimes I miss them so much I physically ache."

4. "Maybe I'm losing my perspective," commented Pat, "but my teenagers make me feel like every decision I make is intended to make them miserable. I

wish just once someone would say to them, 'Listen to your mother; she's right.' "

5. "I can't shake this overwhelming sense of responsibility. My child is totally dependent on me for everything. I am so afraid I won't be able to give him everything he genuinely needs."

6. "Every decision I make is based on money. It's really hard for me to buy anything that's 'just for me' because the whole family is making huge financial sacrifices since the divorce," laments Krista.

God has good news for parents. He loves us each very much—so much that He gave His only Son to live, die, and rise again in order to earn for us forgiveness of sins, eternal salvation, and the strength and power to start over, trusting in His promises.

Promises from God

Work in small groups to read each of the following promises from God and apply each promise to the needs and concerns of parents—especially parents who are raising their children alone.

1. If You, O LORD, kept a record of sins, O Lord, who could stand? But with You there is forgiveness; therefore You are feared. I wait for the LORD, my soul waits, and in His Word I put my hope. O Israel, put your hope in the LORD, for with the LORD is unfailing love and with Him is full redemption. He Himself will redeem Israel from all their sins (Psalm 130:3–5, 7–8).

2. "Come to Me, all you who are weary and burdened, and I will give you rest" (Matthew 11:28).

3. He will not let your foot slip—He who watches over you will not slumber. The LORD will keep you from all harm—He will watch over your life (Psalm 121:3, 7).

4. The LORD will guide you always; He will satisfy your needs in a sun-scorched land and will strengthen your frame. You will be like a well-watered garden, like a spring whose waters never fail. Your people will rebuild the ancient ruins and will raise up the age-old foundations; you will be called Repairer of Broken Walls, Restorer of Streets with Dwellings (Isaiah 58:11–12).

11

5. No, in all these things we are more than conquerors through Him who loved us. For I am convinced that neither death nor life, neither angels nor demons, neither the present nor the future, nor any powers, neither height nor depth, nor anything else in all creation, will be able to separate us from the love of God that is in Christ Jesus our Lord (Romans 8:37–39).

For Reflection

1. For what reasons might single parents judge themselves harshly? Why might others look down upon a parent who is single?

2. When Jesus heard that John the Baptist had been killed by King Herod, He withdrew by boat privately to a solitary place. But when the crowds followed Him, His love for them moved Him to heal their sick and later to provide them with a miraculous meal. Only later was Jesus able to withdraw to be by Himself to talk to His heavenly Father in prayer (Matthew 14:13–23).

What help does God provide His people when they are emersed in a fury of stress-producing activities and situations? when they just need to be alone?

God's Love Makes a Difference

By faith, God in Christ has made us new people with new opportunities to begin again. Now, through God's Word, His Spirit continues to work in our lives, making us more into the type of people God would have us be. In Philippians 4:8 God encourages His people to stress in their lives, "Whatever is true, whatever is noble, whatever is right, whatever is pure, whatever is lovely, whatever is admirable ... excellent or praise worthy. . . ."

Looking at things in a positive way turns negative thoughts and feelings into the positive outlook and outcomes from which both we and those around us will benefit. Practice turning negative thoughts and conclusions into positive ones, in the exercise below. The first two are done for you.

Negative Thought	Positive Response
I am a failure.	I do a lot of things well.
I am all alone.	I enjoy being alone at times.
No one loves me.	
I can't do everything on my list of things to do.	
I won't reach out to strangers; they wouldn't like me.	
My kids don't want me to date.	

Adapted from *I Didn't Plan to Be a Single Parent* by Bobbie Reed (St. Louis: CPH 1981).

▼

To Do at Home

As God's Spirit moves us to reach out with the love of Jesus to others who need our love, concern, and support, we can encourage them to lift their eyes to Christ as we help to lift their spirits by showing God's love for them.

Consider each of the following ways the love of Jesus may touch your life. Then consider all ways Christ's love may come into the lives of others through you. Check all that may apply in both lists.

I Can ...

_____trust in God's promises to never leave me, to always love me, and to help me with the challenges I face.

_____refresh myself with His comfort and power by reading and meditating on His Word and receiving the Sacrament regularly.

_____take things one step at a time, making one positive change in my life today.

_____seek the support, companionship, and encouragement of those who accept me because, by faith, I too am a child of God.

_____leave the hurt from the past behind and forgive those who have offended me just as God in Christ has forgiven me, knowing that while forgiveness cannot change the past, it can change my future.

I Can ...

_____ 1. begin and/or support a food pantry, clothing exchange, and/or financial assistance effort in my congregation or community for those who may be in need.

_____ 2. share clothes my children have outgrown with parents of young children.

_____ 3. encourage and support my congregation in its programs and outreach efforts aimed specifically at single parents.

_____ 4. plan and take specific steps to make single parents feel welcome at church-related activities.

_____ 5. provide or organize free baby-sitting for single parents who need some time for themselves.

Closing Prayer

Dear Lord, thank You for Your love for us. Help and encourage us as we share Your love with those around us, beginning with those in our families. In Jesus' name we pray. Amen.

2

Meeting My Children's Needs

Opening Prayer

Thank You, loving Father, for the light of the Gospel You have given us to through Your Son, Jesus Christ. Help us to be Your lights so we may bring the warmth and illumination only You can provide to our children and to all others whose lives we touch. In Jesus' name we pray. Amen.

Focusing Our Attention

Rank order each of the following according to their popularity among the members of your family. Share and explain your ranking to a partner or the others in your small group.

_____attending a ball game as a family

_____a family picnic

_____a family vacation

_____Thanksgiving at Grandma's

_____family movie or video night

The Love of a Parent

God's design provides for children to be born to parents who will love and care for them. But because of sin, many children live in an environment in which they are unwanted, mistreated, or ignored. These children may have two parents, one parent, or no parents. Referring to the plight of these children, a convention speaker once remarked, "Fortunate is any child who knows the love of a parent."

But God our heavenly Father loves all children—just as He loves all people of all ages. Comment on the love of God for children as you see it expressed in each of the following Bible verses.

1. For You created my inmost being; You knit me together in my mother's womb. I praise You because I am fearfully and wonderfully made; Your works are wonderful, I know that full well. My frame was not hidden from You when I was made in the secret place. When I was woven together in the depths of the earth, Your eyes saw my unformed body. All the days ordained for me were written in Your book before one of them came to be (Psalm 139:13–16).

2. For [God] choose us in [Christ Jesus] before the creation of the world to be holy and blameless in His sight. In love He predestined us to be adopted as His sons [and daughters] through Jesus Christ, in accordance with His pleasure and will—to the praise of His glorious grace, which He has freely given us in the One he loves (Ephesians 1:4–6).

3. I will pour out My Spirit on your offspring, and My blessing on your descendants. They will spring up like grass in a meadow, like poplar trees by flowing streams (Isaiah 44:3b–4).

17
▼

4. [Jesus] said to them, "Let the little children come to Me, and do not hinder them, for the kingdom of heaven belongs to such as these." And He took the children in His arms, put His hands on them and blessed them (Mark 10:14b, 16).

5. He decreed statutes for Jacob and established the law in Israel, which He commanded our forefathers to teach their children, so the next generation would know them, even the children yet to be born, and they in turn would tell their children. Then they would put their trust in God (Psalm 78:5–7a).

6. His name is the Lord. ... A father to the fatherless, a defender of widows, is God in His holy dwelling. God sets the lonely in families (Psalm 68:4–6a).

7. And your sons [and daughters] will be taught by the LORD, and great will be your children's peace (Isaiah 54:13).

For the Children

Despite our sinfulness, God continues to love us. He demonstrated that love by sending His Son to live, die, and rise again for the sins of people everywhere. In Jesus God offers forgiveness, eternal life, and a new beginning in a life that honors Him.

No parent needs ever to feel that he or she must parent alone. God promises help, joy, and peace to all who place their trust in Him. After all, no matter how much any parent loves his or her child, God loves that child even more.

Look for evidence of God's presence and power in the following poem written by a single parent.

Our Son

Our son is quite a work of art;
He's growing rapidly.
He was born once to the two of us
Now he's God's—forgiven, free.

He has my eyes; he has my nose.
He gets his smile from you.
And his amused yet puzzled grin—
He gets that from you, too.

He asks about you now and then.
I tell him all I can—
Of the good in you I see in him
As he grows to be a man.

(anonymous)

1. Tell how God's love can be seen in this single parent's attitude toward his or her son: toward the boy's other parent.

2. What words in the poem describe God's working of the saving faith in a human life?

3. Comment on the atmosphere you would expect to find if you were to meet this single parent and son in their home.

God's Power for Parenting

As God's people receive the strength, guidance, and hope He provides in His holy Word, He helps us to face the challenges and stresses of our own families as He moves us to reach out to others to help and encourage them in the struggles they face.

You are about to meet several parents. As you learn about them and their family situations, look for implied or expressed needs. Ask yourself what you might say or do to share the love of Jesus in each situation.

Meet Steve.

Steve's wife died after a decade of deteriorating health. While he felt prepared for her death when it finally came, he now suspects that his two teenage sons never really thought their mother was going to die. After an initial period of grieving, Steve believes he is coping well and is looking forward to making a new life. In fact, he feels that an enormous burden has been lifted, although he hesitates to admit to his sons how difficult the prolonged illness was for him to handle. His sons appear to resent their father's peace of mind.

1. What fears or feelings may the boys be acting upon—either openly or by their attitudes?

2. What assurances do the boys need from their father?

3. What might have been done to help Steve's sons be better prepared for their mother's death?

4. If this family belonged to your congregation, how could you help them?

Meet Jeanne.

Jeanne believes she is doing a good job of raising Kyle, who was born the year after she graduated from high school. Everyone told her it would be difficult—impossible, some said—to raise a healthy, happy child when she had no money, no job, and no family to turn to for help. But she is doing it! Today she has a good job, satisfactory day-care arrangements for Kyle, and a future that looks encouraging.

Now that Kyle has started school, though, a whole new problem has arisen. Kyle is making friends easily and He is learning about other families. Now he is asking the question Jeanne had always dreaded: "Where's my dad?"

"I guess I'm just going to have to tell him the truth," Jeanne says. "His father was a bum. Kyle needs to know the truth."

1. What does Kyle need to know about his father? How do you think Jeanne should answer Kyle's question?

2. If you were Kyle's Sunday school teacher and you were trying to teach the class about the loving relationship we have with our heavenly Father, how might Kyle's situation affect the way you taught the lesson?

3. How does your congregation respond to children born out of wedlock? How comfortable does the new mother feel in the congregational setting? Assess your congregation's attitudes honestly and discuss improvements that might be made.

Meet Darrell.

Darrell has full custody of his six-year-old daughter, Nicole. His ex-wife abandoned them when Nicole was just an infant. "Sometimes I think I'm doing real well," says Darrell. "In fact, I've surprised myself at the things I've learned to do. But every once in a while Nicole throws something new at me, such as, 'Daddy, will you put my hair in pigtails?' or 'Will I be able to have babies someday?' That's when I become aware of how desperately she needs a female influence in her life. She needs so much that I can't give her."

1. If Darrell expressed his concerns to you, what could you tell him that would make him feel more confident about his parenting skills? What kinds of positive suggestions could you offer him?

2. In what ways might your congregation be able to assist Darrell in providing "a mother's touch" for Nicole? in helping other single-parent families?

To Do at Home

1. Parenting requires attending to each of the following three areas. Ask God's continued guidance and direction on your future. Plan a goal to improve your life in one or more of these areas beginning this week.

Financial Resources (Are there corners I could cut, a plan for generating extra income I or my children might generate?)

Household Management (Could I devise a plan to more effectively involve my children in the household chores? Could I rearrange my schedule to make better use of my time? Does everything I do need to be done or done so often? Could I find a way to simplify this aspect of my life?)

Child Care (Can I trade off baby-sitting times with another household or share a babysitter with another family? How can I improve the time I spend with my children? Could I involve the other parent of my child or other family members in a more significant way?)

2. Set aside time this week with each of your children. During this time together tell him or her directly how much you love him or her and how happy you are that God gave her/him to you. Ask your child about his or her life goals and aspirations. Pray together for God's guidance and blessing on your child's life.

3. Do some significant act of love for each of the following as a response to God for His goodness to you in Christ Jesus:

Yourself

Your child(ren)

Someone outside your family who needs help or encouragement

Closing Prayer

Dear Lord, thank You for loving us and for loving the children You have given us. Lord, we want to do more than survive; we want to excel both as parents and as Your children. Join us in our parenting. Guide and direct us in the attitudes we project and in the relationships we build with our children and with those others who are significant in their lives. Bless us with Your Holy Spirit to live our lives to Your glory. In Jesus' name we pray. Amen.

A New Day ...
A New Start

3

Opening Prayer

Dear Father in heaven, how great is Your forgiving and healing love for us. You cared enough for us in our fallen and hopeless condition to send Your only Son to win us back from sin and its devastating consequences. Thank You, God. Send us Your Holy Spirit now, and help us to trust ever more in You and to be Your people in our feelings and attitudes as well as in the things we say and do. We pray in Jesus' name. Amen.

Focusing Our Attention

Which of the following vehicles best describes how you feel right now? Explain your choice to a partner or to the others in a group of three or four.

_____a decorated limousine

_____a sedan with an overheating engine

_____a race car at the staring line

_____a taxi that has about run out of gas

_____a recreational vehicle, temporarily parked

That Old, Familiar Feeling

One evening while she was making dinner, Mary Williams asked her husband, Herb, to go to the grocery store for a gallon of milk. Herb left for the store but never came home. He was killed on the way in a head-on collision. "If only I had remembered to get some milk earlier in the day," Mary regretted later, "Herb would still be alive."

Guilt is a frequent guest in the lives of practically everyone. It often surfaces from feelings of remorse and blame over deliberate thoughts, actions, or failures. Or it emerges in response to thoughts and feelings that we must somehow be responsible for events and occurrences totally outside our control, as in the case of Mary.

1. Look at the following areas of your life. Think for a moment about the feelings of guilt you have had about each.

Job

Children

Home

Leisure activities

Financial matters

Relatives

2. In Psalm 38, David tells God (and us) about the consequences of sin in his life.

a. After reading verses 4–8 below, list the ways sin has affected David physically, emotionally, and socially.

"My guilt has overwhelmed me like a burden too heavy to bear. My wounds fester and are loathsome because of my sinful folly. I am bowed down and brought very low; all day long I go about mourning.

My back is filled with searing pain; there is no health in my body. I am feeble and utterly crushed; I groan in anguish of heart."

b. What similar consequences of sin do you see in your own life and in the world around you?

3. Even amid the guilt and other consequences of sin in our lives, God is continually working things for our good. He desires these consequences to bring us to recognize the devastation sin has caused. He wants us to see that on our own we are powerless to change our condition. Read verses 15–17 of Psalm 38 printed below.

"I wait for You, O LORD; You will answer, O Lord my God. For I said, 'Do not let them gloat or exalt themselves over me when my foot slips.' For I am about to fall, and my pain is ever with me. I confess my iniquity; I am troubled by my sin."

Even in David's great despair, however, he knows that there is an antidote for his guilt. Of what assurance does David remind himself?

4. God answered David's cry for relief from guilt—and ours. Our heavenly Father graciously sent His Son to forgive us and restore us from the consequences of sin that plague us. Read a portion of another psalm of David, Psalm 103. Write a phrase

beside each of the following verses to summarize the description of God's love provided in that verse.

"⁸The LORD is compassionate and gracious, slow to anger, abounding in love. ⁹He will not always accuse, nor will He harbor His anger forever; ¹⁰He does not treat us as our sins deserve or repay us according to our iniquities. ¹¹For as high as the heavens are above the earth, so great is His love for those who fear Him; ¹²as far as the east is from the west, so far has He removed our transgressions from us. ¹³As a father has compassion on his children, so the Lord has compassion on those who fear Him; ¹⁴for He knows how we are formed, He remembers that we are dust. ¹⁵As for man, his days are like grass, he flourishes like a flower of the field; ¹⁶the wind blows over it and it is gone, and its place remembers it no more. ¹⁷But from everlasting to everlasting the LORD's love is with those who fear Him.

5. God rewards those who love and trust in Him the instant they come to faith. His reward is not just for heaven; it is to be enjoyed on earth, too. In Psalm 51, David expresses his guilt over his adultery with Bathsheba and the chain of sinful events which followed. Consider the following verses:

"⁵Surely I was sinful at birth, sinful from the time my mother conceived me. ⁶Surely You desire truth in the inner parts; You teach me wisdom in the inmost place. ⁷Cleanse me with hyssop, and I will be clean; wash me, and I will be whiter than snow. ⁸Let me hear joy and gladness; let the bones You have crushed rejoice. [9]Hide Your face from my sins and blot out all my iniquity. [10]Create in me a pure heart, O God, and renew a steadfast spirit within me. [11]Do not cast me from Your presence or take Your Holy Spirit from me. [12]Restore to me the joy of Your salvation and grant me a willing spirit, to sustain me. [13]Then I will teach transgressors Your ways and sinners will turn back to You.

a. Draw an arrow pointing upward beside the verse in which David describes himself.

b. Draw an arrow pointing downward beside the verse in which David states God's desire for those He loves.

c. Underline each request David makes of God.

d. Circle the verse that tells of David's planned response to God for His goodness toward him.

Removing the Blanket of Guilt

But God has bridged guilt and wellness by Jesus Christ. Because of all Christ has done for us—His perfect life, His death, and His resurrection—through faith He melts our feelings of blame and self-condemnation and gives us peace, confidence, and hope. As surely as He has forgiven all our sins He desires us to bring our problems, concerns, and regrets and give them all over to Him. He is big enough to carry all our burdens for us.

1. Discuss some of the issues that might be a source of guilt for single parents. How valid are these feelings?

2. What kind of guilt is the psalmist (here, again, it's David) turning over to God in the following verses?

"Remember not the sins of my youth and my rebellious ways; according to Your love remember me, for You are good, O LORD" (Psalm 25:7).

"Who can discern his errors? Forgive my hidden faults" (Psalm 19:12).

3. Why do we sometimes find it difficult to "let go" of sins from our past? Why is it necessary that we forgive ourselves if we trust in God's whole-hearted and complete forgiveness for us in Christ Jesus?

4. According to the following passage, what step should someone take who desires God's complete forgiveness in Christ?

"If we confess our sins, He is faithful and just and will forgive us our sins and purify us from all unrighteousness" (1 John 1:9).

5. Read the following verses and answer the question following each.

a. "Their sins and lawless acts I will remember no more" (Hebrews 10:17).

If we have confessed to God all our sins (the current sins of which we are aware, the sins of our past, and the sins we don't even realize we've committed) trusting in Christ for the forgiveness He has won for us, what has become of those sins?

b. Read the following verse. "This then is how we know that we belong to the truth, and how we set our hearts at rest in His presence whenever our hearts condemn us. For God is greater than our hearts, and He knows everything" (1 John 3:19–20).

What promise does God provide for those who don't feel forgiven?

Forgiven, Restored, Ready to Begin Again

Part of the new life God brings to us involves not only feeling good about ourselves as God's redeemed children but moving forward as God's people, making use of the opportunities God has provided in our daily lives. Paul tells us how to go about it in his letter to the Philippians, "Forgetting what is behind and straining toward what is ahead, I press on toward the prize for which God has called me heavenward in Christ Jesus" (Philippians 3:13–14). Consider the following practical applications of these words from Philippians.

Forgive and Forget

1. Read, reflect, and trust what God's Word tells us about forgiveness.

2. Recognizing what we can and cannot change, work at accepting others as they are.

3. Ask God for the forgiving power of His love in your life.

4. Consciously forgive someone who has hurt you.

5. Take deliberate steps to begin again, creating new experiences and forming new relationships that will provide new memories and new associations.

Press on Toward the Prize

1. Spend time daily in God's Word, thereby maintaining a close relationship with Christ.

2. Become the spiritual leader of your family, seek God's will for the goals and direction of your personal and family life.

3. Develop close relationships with other Christians and involve yourself in the life of your congregation.

4. Entrust your problems and concerns for now and for the future to Him who has promised never to leave and always to care for us.

5. Work at developing a positive attitude that reflects the love of Christ to those within and outside your family. Learn to listen, support, encourage, and care.

The following represent experiences common among single parents. What guidance would you offer each of these parents in dealing with their feelings? Suggest practical solutions to the frustrations they express. Refer to the promises of Scripture that we've already discussed in this lesson.

1. *Carmen's three children are just old enough to begin participating in school and community activities: softball, gymnastics, choir, scouting—the activities seem to be endless. "I feel like I have to be two people," Carmen laments. "I have to prove that I'm a good parent, even though there is just one of me. I feel like I have to go to everything my kids are involved in or other parents will think I don't care or that my chil-*

dren are disadvantaged. The trouble is, there just isn't enough of me to go around."

2. *"By the time Joannie and I agreed that divorce was inevitable," explains Kurt, "I already felt I had done everything I could to hold things together. We'd been to counseling, we'd talked with our pastor, and we'd even tried separating for a while, hoping a fresh start would make things better. I wanted to keep trying, but she decided our marriage couldn't work. Now I'm haunted by thoughts of things I 'could have done.' I just can't let go and get on with life. I feel like I'm really holding my kids back and keeping them from getting on with life, too."*

3. *"It's just been Allie and me for so long now,"* reflects Charlene. *"We did everything together; she's been my whole life for six years. Now I've met Walter and suddenly my life has a whole new dimension I wasn't anticipating. If I'm with Walter, I feel guilty for not being with Allie. If I'm with Allie, I really miss Walter. Wherever I am, I feel guilty."*

To Do at Home

Plan to put into practice one or more of the applications from the "Forgiven, Restored, and Ready to Begin Again" section during the coming week.

Closing Prayer

Close by reading responsively the promises God makes in Isaiah 40:29–31. Give thanks for the comfort these promises give to single parents.

Leader: He gives strength to the weary and increases the power of the weak.

Response: Even youths grow tired and weary, and young men stumble and fall;

Leader: but those who hope in the LORD will renew their strength.

Response: They will soar on wings like eagles;

Leader: they will run and not grow weary,

Response: they will walk and not be faint.

The Single Parent and the Church

4

Opening Prayer

Dear heavenly Father, You have created us to live in community with others. Thank You for the new relationship You have established for us as Your children by faith in Christ Jesus. Fill us with Your Spirit's power so that we may reach out with your love to all others, but especially to our brothers and sisters in Christ. Bless us as we study Your Word today. In Jesus' name we pray. Amen.

Focusing Our Attention

Choose from among the following list of body parts the one that best describes you. Explain your choice to a partner or to the others in a group of three or four.

_____hand

_____eye

_____foot

_____ear

_____mouth

God's Church—The Body of Christ

Paul in his letter to believers in Corinth uses the parts of the human body to describe the fellowship of believers. He writes, "Just as each of us has one body with many members, and these members do not all have the same function, so in Christ we who are many form one body, and each member belongs to all the others" (Romans 12:4–5).

God desires to meet our spiritual, social, and emotional needs through the church. As His Holy Spirit works through the Gospel, He strengthens our faith, forgives our sins, and empowers us for our daily challenges. Through the fellowship of believers, God helps us bear one another's burdens; He comforts us, reaching out with someone else's hands to assure us that He loves us.

Single parents sometimes feel that the church and the people in it have let them down—often during the time of their initial crisis. Does God fail? Never. Do His people fail? Often. Is there forgiveness for our failures? Consider it done! God's only Son earned the forgiveness for all sins through His life, death, and resurrection.

When you think of a "perfect church," what are some of the characteristics that come to mind? Friendly? Inclusive? Forgiving? Understanding? Welcoming? Surely these are all important. As members of a body of which Christ Himself is the head, we would each like to believe that we can *be* all of these things to our fellow church members. Plus, we hope that our own needs will be met by the abundance of these gifts when we, too, find ourselves in need of them.

Read together the description St. Paul gives of the "perfect church" in Colossians 3:12–17:

"Therefore, as God's chosen people, holy and dearly loved, clothe yourselves with compassion, kindness, humility, gentleness and patience. Bear with each other and forgive whatever grievances you may have against one another. Forgive as the Lord forgave you. And over all these virtues put on love, which binds them all together in perfect unity.

"Let the peace of Christ rule in your hearts, since as members of one body you were called to peace. And be thankful. Let the word of Christ dwell in you richly as you teach and admonish one another with all wisdom, and as you sing psalms, hymns and spiritual songs with gratitude in your hearts to God. And whatever you do, whether in word or deed, do it all in the name of the Lord Jesus, giving thanks to God the Father through him."

1. What are some of the characteristics God desires to see evidenced in the lives of members of the church?

2. Share some evidences of these virtues found in your congregation.

3. One of the comments often made inside and outside the church is that the church is too "family-oriented." How would you suggest the church respond to that accusation?

4. What further insight into the role of the church do you find in the following passage from Ephesians?

"Consequently, you are no longer foreigners and aliens, but fellow citizens with God's people and members of God's household, built on the foundation of the apostles and prophets, with Christ Jesus Himself as

▼

the chief cornerstone. In Him the whole building is joined together and rises to become a holy temple in the Lord. And in Him you too are being built together to become a dwelling in which God lives by His Spirit" (Ephesians 2:19–22).

5. How might those seeking to grow as faithful church members apply the following passage?

"Do not let any unwholesome talk come out of your mouths, but only what is helpful for building others up according to their needs, that it may benefit those who listen. And do not grieve the Holy Spirit of God, with whom you were sealed for the day of redemption. Get rid of all bitterness, rage and anger, brawling and slander, along with every form of malice. Be kind and compassionate to one another, forgiving each other, just as in Christ God forgave you. Be imitators of God, therefore, as dearly loved children and live a life of love, just as Christ loved us and gave Himself up for us as a fragrant offering and sacrifice to God" (Ephesians 4:29–5:2).

Communicating Our Needs to Each Other

Although God knows what our deepest thoughts and needs are without our having to express them,

He did not give us the same ability to see into the hearts of others. Therefore we often fail each other—not because we plan to be unresponsive, but because we don't know what is expected of us or how to express what needs to be said or done.

The following frustrations were expressed by single parents who are members of congregations very much like yours. They are sitting in the pew next to you, teaching your children in Sunday school, and making phone calls to remind you of Friendship Sunday. They've been hurt deeply, but by God's grace they've found a place among God's people once again.

Listen to what they have to say and discuss what you could do, either individually or as a congregation, to minister to others who may be experiencing these same hurts. If you have experienced some of these feelings, ask yourself how you might have done a better job of conveying your needs to your congregation and pastor.

1. Melanie: *Sundays were awful when I was pregnant with Joey. The people in my congregation didn't know what to say to me or to my parents. All of us pretended nothing was happening. After Joey was born, lots of people made a big fuss over him. But nobody ever acknowledged how difficult it had been for me to come to church while I was pregnant and in high school. It was like once Joey was born everything was "normal," but before he was born nobody knew what to say. Actually, things haven't been "normal" for me for a long time.*

a. Why do you think everybody "pretended nothing was happening" while Melanie was pregnant?

b. How do fellow members of a congregation minister effectively to a young woman who is pregnant and single? How can they best relate to her after the baby is born?

2. Cal: *I needed to go to church; I needed something stable and familiar in my life. But I wanted to just slip in and slip out. It hurt so much to be there alone, without my kids. I couldn't handle talking with people, even though most of them meant well when they asked how I was doing. It would have been easy just to quit going.*

a. Jesus once said, "It is not the healthy who need a doctor, but the sick." Explain Jesus' words in light of Cal's situation.

b. Judging from Cal's words, how could members of his congregation best help him during this difficult time?

3. Miranda: *I really felt like the church let me down. My friends suddenly seemed uncomfortable when I was around them. I called them when I needed to talk, but it would have meant so much to me if they had called me—just to ask how I was doing. My son needed to feel that somebody at church cared about his pain too. We ended up going to another church*

where nobody knew everything that had happened to us.

a. Putting the best construction on everything, why may Miranda's friends have suddenly felt uncomfortable around her?

b. What might Miranda have learned from this situation that will equip her for future Christian service?

4. Ruth: *My husband wasn't a member of my church. So when we were divorced, I didn't tell anyone what was happening—not even my pastor. I didn't want anyone to know how much I hurt or how hopeless my financial situation seemed. I just kept going to church, trying to put up a brave front.*

a. How might Ruth have better dealt with her situation?

b. What was good about the way Ruth handled her situation?

▼

5. Damon: *The congregation and the pastor were wonderful to us while Elyse was dying of cancer. Many members visited regularly, brought meals, and stayed with the kids while I was at the hospital. By the time Elyse died, many of these members had become like family to me. After the funeral, though, they stopped coming. In a sense, I needed them more then than I did while Elyse was still alive.*

a. If you were Damon, how could you best deal with your disappointment at the lack of love and care demonstrated after Elyse's death?

b. What helpful insight does Damon's experience provide for you?

Reaffirming God's Challenge

Most of us, as care-givers and care-seekers, have at times disappointed each other. As we ask God's help in being more sensitive to the needs of our brothers and sisters in the faith, we consider St. Paul's challenge to the church at Philippi as recorded in Philippians 2:1–4:

"If you have any encouragement from being united with Christ, if any comfort from His love, if any fellowship with the Spirit, if any tenderness and compassion, then make my joy complete by being like-minded, having the same love, being one in spirit and purpose. Do nothing out of selfish ambition or vain conceit, but in humility consider others better than yourselves. Each of you should look not only to your own interests, but also to the interests of others."

1. Apply the above words to those desiring to provide support and encouragement to one another.

2. What are some actions you could take right now to make your congregation more responsive to the needs of single-parent families?

3. What activities and ministries of your congregation may especially benefit from the leadership and involvement of single parents?

To Do at Home

Consider yourself as each of the parts of the body referred to in "Focusing Our Attention." Plan one way you can share God's love in Christ with some other member of Christ's body during the coming week. Then put your plans into action.

hand

eye

foot

ear

mouth

Closing Prayer

Conclude your study using the following litany. If you designate a special Sunday to celebrate the triumphs of single parents and pray for God's grace and help in their times of struggle, you might suggest to your pastor that a litany such as this be part of your service.

Leader: Heavenly Father, thank You for being the Father on whom we can depend to meet our needs, heal our hurts, and embrace us with love that is more eager to forgive than to judge.

Response: Help us to remember that when our human relationships fail to meet the standards you have set, it is not You who has failed, but us.

Leader: Remind us that for every disappointment You provide hope; for every broken heart You pour out healing; and for every failure You offer forgiveness through Your Son, Jesus Christ.

Response: Thank You for the family You provide for us through our congregation and those with whom we meet to share and study Your Word.

Leader: Keep us mindful of those among us who are struggling with heartaches and concerns that are unknown to us.

Response: Help us to be eager to respond when our kind words may bring comfort; when our gift of time may lighten someone's load; when the blessings You have so generously provided us may ease a child's want; when our arms may encircle the lonely with Your love.

Leader: Give us strength to carry out your command to love one another and to bear each other's burdens.

Response: For we know, Lord, that You will not ask us to do more for someone else than You have already done for us.

Leader: Thank you for our gift of faith.

Response: May it ever sustain us, build us up, and allow us to live in the joyous expectation of reaching our eternal home with You in heaven. In the name of Jesus we pray. Amen.

5
Forward with Jesus

Opening Prayer

Dear Father in heaven, thank You for Your constant, unending care. We know that You love us and our children with a greater than human care and love. You always remain with us, encouraging and renewing us in the faith as You refresh us in the knowledge that in Christ Jesus we are Your people, forgiven and free. Bless our study today. Equip us with Your Spirit's power so that we may trust more fully in You as we anticipate the good things You have in store for us. We pray in Jesus' name. Amen.

Focusing Our Attention

Choose one song title from among the following that best describes a recent event or mood in your family. Explain your choice to a partner or to those in your group.

Singin' in the Rain

I'm a Believer

By the Light of the Silvery Moon

Bridge Over Troubled Waters

I'll Be Seeing You

One Fine Day

Hound Dog

I Want to Hold Your Hand

Sounds of Silence

In the Shade of the Old Apple Tree

Breaking Through—with God's Help

Have you ever been lost in a maze of highways or country roads? As you make turns onto unfamiliar roads, panic or annoyance take over, rendering you unable to make logical, rational decisions about how to free yourself from your dilemma. Then, quite unexpectedly, you turn onto a road or see a landmark that is familiar. Suddenly you know where you are. You know everything is going to be okay. Your journey can continue.

Single parents often describe "break through" experiences in their journey along the dual roads of singleness and parenthood. Something happens—perhaps a single event or merely a passage of time—that makes what seemed an impossible journey suddenly possible. In this session we are going to examine what some single parents have shared as "break though" points in their journey.

Read together Isaiah 42:16:

"I will lead the blind by ways they have not known, along unfamiliar paths I will guide them; I will turn the darkness into light before them and make the rough places smooth. These are the things I will do; I will not forsake them."

▼

1. Share with the class a time when you felt forsaken by God. What made you realize that He had not abandoned you, that He was still in control?

2. God uses the phrase "I will" five times in the passage above from Isaiah. Underline the five specific things He promises He will do.

From Grief to Acceptance

"I finally came to accept that things would never be the same again," said one young mother several years after her divorce. *"I did not want my marriage to end, but once I realized I couldn't change reality, I was able to go on. It took a couple of years for me to do that."*

Although death is usually regarded as the ultimate grief, most acknowledge that many situations in life require working through a grieving process. When plunged into a grievous situation, initially we can't see a way out. We may feel God has abandoned us. We may believe we will never experience joy again.

In a classic analysis of grief, *On Death and Dying* (New York: Macmillan Co, 1969), Elizabeth Kubler-Ross broke the grieving process into five stages. Kubler-Ross contends that a person must pass through these stages in order to progress from grief to acceptance. The stages are not all the same length, nor are they necessarily experienced in the order presented.

While Dr. Kubler-Ross was primarily discussing grief over the loss of a loved one by death, her analysis has frequently been applied to any major loss we might experience. Divorce, a house fire, an unexpected job transfer or loss, or a child who becomes addicted to drugs or alcohol will force us into a grieving process as we struggle to deal with the loss of something important in our lives. Kubler-Ross' stages are described as follows.

Stage 1: Denial. Often when receiving shocking news, the mind cushions itself against unpleasantness by refusing to believe that something is true. Persons in this stage may reason as follows. "I don't believe she's having an affair." "I can't possibly be pregnant." "I know this isn't happening; I know I'll wake up and find out I'm dreaming." "I don't care what the doctor says, I know I'll walk again."

Stage 2: Anger. Angry responses might include, "How could you do this to me?" or "Why do these things always happen to me?" Sometimes this anger is directed toward another person; sometimes it's directed at God. At other times the anger has no particular object.

Stage 3: Bargaining. This can be so subtle that the grieving person doesn't realize he or she is trying to "make a deal." Someone in this stage may reason, "Maybe if I keep the house cleaner, he won't leave me." "If I quit my job to take care of her, she won't die." Children (who also grieve) are especially overt in this stage: "If I'm really good, Mom and Dad might get back together again."

Stage 4: Depression. For some people, this can be such a debilitating stage that they are unable to progress to wholeness. The feeling of "not being able to go on" may last for a few weeks or for years.

Stage 5: Acceptance. Note that there's a huge difference between acceptance and agreement. Although a person in this stage may never be able to say, "I'm glad this happened." Once healing has begun, however, he or she can rejoice in the strength God has provided, in the emotional and spiritual growth he or she has gained, and in the comfort that comes from knowing that God does not abandon us, even in our darkest moments. That is what St. Paul meant when he said in 1 Thessalonians 5:18, "Give thanks in all circumstances."

1. If you are a single parent, can you determine where in the "grieving process" you are?

2. What comfort does the following passage from Isaiah give us in our journey toward acceptance?

"But now, this is what the LORD says—He who created you, O Jacob, He who formed you, O Israel: 'Fear not, for I have redeemed you; I have summoned you by name; you are Mine. When you pass through the waters, I will be with you; and when you pass through the rivers, they will not sweep over you. When you walk through the fire, you will not be burned; the flames will not set you ablaze. For I am the LORD, your God, the Holy One of Israel, your Savior" (Isaiah 43:1–3a).

3. In our initial hurt, we may not see that God's ultimate plan is not only to heal us, but to give us an opportunity. Read 2 Corinthians 1:3–4 printed below and explain.

"Praise be to the God and Father of our Lord Jesus Christ, the Father of compassion and the God of all comfort, who comforts us in all our troubles, so that we can comfort those in any trouble with the comfort we ourselves have received from God."

From "I Can't" to "I Can"

"When Jeff died, I kept telling myself, 'I can't do this; I know I can't do this.' Then one day it struck me, 'I can do this. I've got to do this.' Things got a lot easier after that."

Many studies have proven the benefit of "positive thinking." Often patients who believe they can get better and want to do so recover dramatically. Addictions can be overcome, marriages can be saved, and jobs can be found when we say, "I know I can do this." But those who trust in Jesus as their Savior have more than positive thinking operating on their behalf. They know and believe that He who went willingly to the cross to earn their forgiveness and eternal life and salvation has all the power and authority of the entire universe at His disposal. How blest the Christian is to say "I can" and know that God is the force behind that affirmation!

1. How might a person who is torn between "I can't" and "I can" in some area of his or her life benefit from regularly repeating and meditating on the following verse from Philippians, "I can do everything through Him who gives Me strength" (4:13).

2. Why, according to the following passage, is Paul convinced that he can do all things through Christ?

"But He said to me, 'My grace is sufficient for you, for My power is made perfect in weakness.' Therefore I will boast all the more gladly about my weaknesses, so that Christ's power may rest on me" (2 Corinthians 12:9).

3. St. Paul's prayer for the people in the church at Ephesus is printed as follows. What particular phrase in that prayer means the most to you?

"For this reason I kneel before the Father, from whom His whole family in heaven and on earth derives its name. I pray that out of His glorious riches He may strengthen you with power through His Spirit in your inner being, so that Christ may dwell in your hearts through faith. And I pray that you, being rooted and established in love, may have power, together with all the saints, to grasp how wide and long and high and deep is the love of Christ, and to know this love that surpasses knowledge—that you may be filled to the measure of all the fullness of God.

"Now to Him who is able to do immeasurably more than all we ask or imagine, according to His power that is at work within us, to Him be glory in the church and in Christ Jesus throughout all generations, for ever and ever. Amen" (Ephesians 3:14–21).

The Need for Help

"I always thought it was a sign of weakness to go for counseling. Then I realized that just acknowledging the need for help is a sign of strength. Counseling was enormously helpful to me and to my children. Even making the commitment to start counseling was a turning point for us."

The success of professional counseling varies widely. Numerous factors make for success: The determination of those being counseled to make it work, a "good match" between counselor and client, openness and honesty, and a realistic setting of goals by both the counselor and client.

If you have considered professional assistance in dealing with relationships in your life, your pastor or a friend who has been helped may offer valuable suggestions for getting started.

1. How important do you believe it is to receive help from a *Christian* counselor?

2. What counsel does the following selection from James offer to those seeking answers?

"If any of you lacks wisdom, he should ask God, who gives generously to all without finding fault, and it will be given to him. But when he asks, he must believe and not doubt, because he who doubts is like a wave of the sea, blown and tossed by the wind. That man should not think he will receive anything from the Lord; he is a double-minded man, unstable in all he does" (1:5–8).

Dating and a New Beginning

"It took me awhile to want to date after I became single, but even when I thought I was ready I found the whole process uncomfortable and unsatisfactory. When I was finally able to say, 'I want a partner, not just a dad for my kids,' I was able to focus and become more relaxed about dating."

Entire books have been written about the re-entry into the world of dating after becoming single. If a single parent determines he or she is ready to date, complicated feelings and relationships are likely to develop. Practical problems such as paying for a baby-sitter, spending time away from children who have come to expect a parent to "always be there," feeling comfortable with children who might become stepchildren, and desperation over "not making a mistake" add further pressure.

Often the input single parents get from their children is neither helpful nor honest.

1. What help does the following verse give for choosing and developing new relationships?

▲▲▲▲▲▲▲▲▲▲▲▲▲▲▲▲▲▲▲▲▲▲▲▲▲▲▲▲▲

"Do not conform any longer to the pattern of this world, but be transformed by the renewing of your mind. Then you will be able to test and approve what God's will is—His good, pleasing and perfect will" (Romans 12:2).

▼▼▼▼▼▼▼▼▼▼▼▼▼▼▼▼▼▼▼▼▼▼▼▼▼▼▼▼▼

2. According to the following passage, what means does God sometimes use to speak His Word to us? What does that tell us about the friends we spend time with? About relationships we may be interested in pursuing

▲▲▲▲▲▲▲▲▲▲▲▲▲▲▲▲▲▲▲▲▲▲▲▲▲▲▲▲▲▲▲

"Let the word of Christ dwell in you richly as you teach and admonish one another with all wisdom, and as you sing psalms, hymns and spiritual songs with gratitude in your hearts to God" (Colossians 3:16).

▼▼▼▼▼▼▼▼▼▼▼▼▼▼▼▼▼▼▼▼▼▼▼▼▼▼▼▼▼▼

From Grief to Joy

"I thought I'd never laugh again."

Earlier we talked about moving from grief to acceptance. There's more! We may never become joyful about some of the circumstances of our life. That doesn't mean, however, that we will never again know joy. With acceptance comes the ability to move on with our lives. And as we move on, we are open to the many, many joys God still has planned for us.

Read John 16:21–22 printed below.

▲▲▲▲▲▲▲▲▲▲▲▲▲▲▲▲▲▲▲▲▲▲▲▲▲▲▲▲▲▲▲

"A woman giving birth to a child has pain because her time has come; but when her baby is born she forgets the anguish because of her joy that a child is born into the world. So with you: Now is your time of grief, but I will see you again and you will rejoice, and no one will take away your joy."

▼▼▼▼▼▼▼▼▼▼▼▼▼▼▼▼▼▼▼▼▼▼▼▼▼▼▼▼▼▼

▼

1. Shortly before Jesus was arrested and killed, He explained to His disciples what was about to occur. They didn't understand all that He said, and they probably didn't believe how deeply grieved they would be. What did Jesus promise His disciples would happen to them eventually?

2. Since we, too, have been claimed by Christ Jesus through His life, death, and resurrection for us, we know that joy awaits us ... here on earth and in heaven. List three good things that have happened in your life, as God has continued blessing you in the midst of the challenges and struggles of single parenting.

To Do at Home

Think about and/or share something joyful that happened to you this week. Thank God for it.

Closing Prayer

Dear Lord, strengthen us with power through Your Spirit in our inner being, so that Christ may dwell in our hearts through faith. May we, being rooted and established in love, have power, together with all the saints, to grasp how wide and long and high and deep is the love of Christ, and to know this love that surpasses knowledge—that we may be filled to the measure of all the fullness of God.

Now to Him who is able to do immeasurably more than all we ask or imagine, according to His power that is at work within us, to Him be glory in the church and in Christ Jesus throughout all generations, for ever and ever! Amen.

Leader Notes

▲▲▲▲▲▲▲▲▲▲▲▲▲▲▲▲▲▲▲▲▲▲▲▲▲▲▲▲▲▲▲▲

To the Leader:

This study provides much opportunity for open-ended discussion. It will be important to keep the class moving and focused on the material. Encourage participants, especially single parents, to express their opinions and insights. Be sensitive for signals that your congregation needs an on-going ministry to single parents.

While the simple answer to all of our earthly struggles is to "trust in God," as Christians we are called upon to be the physical extension of Christ's body, the church. This study strongly challenges the participants to "get involved" in ministry to single-parent families. If some members of the class display a keen interest in this subject or are willing to organize some of the suggested responses, make certain that the appropriate board or staff person is notified of this interest so that encouragement can be given to proceed.

▼▼▼▼▼▼▼▼▼▼▼▼▼▼▼▼▼▼▼▼▼▼▼▼▼▼▼▼▼▼▼▼

Session 1

Meeting My Needs

▲ Focus

Welcome everyone. Give each participant a copy of the Study Guide. Encourage participants to write their names on the front covers. Ask that they take the booklets home between sessions and bring them back each time the group meets.

▲ Objectives

That by the power of the Holy Spirit working through God's Word the participants will

1. contrast and compare single parenting to parenting in a two-parent household;

2. express a desire to trust in God and His promises as they consider their needs and concerns as parents;

3. demonstrate the peace, power, and joy Christ provides in their parenting and in every other aspect of their lives;

4. reflect on the power of God's love and forgiveness in their lives and dedicate themselves to sharing His love with others.

▲ Opening Prayer

Invite participants to join you in asking God's blessing upon the study of this course, praying the words of the prayer included in the Study Guide.

▲ Focusing Our Attention

Comment on the enormity of the parenting responsibility and that God designed the parenting task to be undertaken by two people. Sin, death, and broken relationships have left some people to champion this demanding task without a spouse. Nevertheless, those who trust in Jesus as their Savior are never alone in anything they do, including single parenting. Jesus, our Savior, will remain with us to help, encourage, and fortify us, enabling us to find our pride, purpose, and self-worth in Him and to share His love with our children and others.

Ask participants to introduce themselves and their families to the others in the group as they share the movie title from the list that reminds them of their life with their children during the past week. If the group is large, you may choose to form two or three smaller groups so the activity will take less time.

▲ Going It Alone

Read the opening paragraph and the scenario to the group. Make certain the class considers all the circumstances under which a parent might become a single parent (divorce, death, never married). Have participants work with partners or in small groups to list similarities and differences between single-parent and two-parent households. Then reassemble as a whole group and make a master list on the board or a large piece of newsprint.

Possible similarities between single-and two-parent households may include interaction between parent, child, and home in which Christ is or is not the head; both may or may not be headed by adults who parent effectively; both contain parents and children with needs, desire, goals, and ambitions.

Possible differences include: single-parent households have only one person who parent; single households may struggle with issues resulting from the death or dissolution of a relationship with the absent parent; single-parent families don't struggle with differences in parenting styles among parents; children in single-parent families may feel compelled to grow up more quickly; single parents don't have the support, encouragement, and counsel of a spouse; single parents may be misunderstood or regarded as dysfunctional because of their nontraditional configuration. Continue with the next section.

▲ What's Happening to Me?

Invite a participant to read the section about Ellen aloud to the group. Then continue with the thoughts expressed in the following paragraphs. Ask participants to work in groups to isolate the needs expressed in the numbered items of the activity. After 5–10 minutes reassemble the whole group and briefly review each. Possible responses follow.

1. Kate seems to feel that she is being judged by others. She already judges herself too harshly. Kate needs affirmation.

2. This parent desires a brief time out from the responsibilities of parenting but can't get a baby-sitter for this purpose. This parent needs time for herself/himself.

3. This parent misses his or her children. He or she desires to play a greater role in their lives.

4. This mother desires support and affirmation of her parenting.

5. Fear and a sense of being totally consumed by his or

her role as a parent are shared by this person. This parent needs reassurance.

6. Krista talks of her financial struggles since her divorce. Krista needs assurance that her needs are important and that it's all right to meet her needs responsibly.

Ask participants how many of these needs and concerns may also be expressed by persons parenting in a two-parent family. Conclude this section emphasizing the Gospel promise of God's forgiving, encouraging, and empowering love for us in Christ Jesus our Lord.

▲ Promises from God

Invite participants to work in small groups to apply these promises of God to the needs and concerns of parents. Review responses briefly as a whole group. Summaries of these passages are as follows.

1. All of us are sinners, but God is the forgiver of sins. He invites us to hope in Him.

2. God invites us to give all of our burdens and worries over to Him; He will provide rest.

3. God's guiding and protecting care never stops, day or night.

Psalm 121 promises that God will "watch over your life" (v. 7) "both now and forevermore" (v. 8). God sees farther ahead (all the way to heaven, in fact) than we can see. Some of our self-imposed responsibilities are really in God's hands far more than we allow them to be.

4. God promises to repair our households, inside and out.

Isaiah 58:11–12 can be especially comforting to single parents because it refers to God's ability to rebuild what the parent may perceive as a "ruined" family. Mention that it may not be God's plan for some people to be ever financially secure. To God, that is not of primary importance. Too much emphasis on material things may distract us from the real goals God has for us. However, because it is so easy for cares of this world to pull Christians away from God instead of toward Him (as He intends), God's love also prompts us to help those who struggle.

5. Nothing will be able to separate us from God and His love for us in Christ Jesus our Lord and Savior. God promises to uphold us spiritually, but He does not promise that we won't go through great trials while living on earth. Empha-

size that God does not "do" terrible things to us. He allows sin to take its course in our lives, but that does not mean that when unpleasant things happen to us He is punishing us. (Christ died once on the cross for all sin.) No matter what happens to us, we cannot be separated spiritually from God unless we choose to estrange ourselves from God.

For Reflection

Discuss the questions in this section as a whole group.

1. Feelings of guilt or the overwhelming sense of responsibility at the task that is solely theirs may lead single parents to judge themselves harshly. Others might look down on single parents, either consciously or unconsciously judging them as failures who are somehow responsible for the situation in which they find themselves.

2. Jesus, too, needed to "get away from it all." Note that Jesus' goal in getting away was to spend time with His Father in prayer. God's peace can comfort and sustain us even when we are in the most stressful and demanding of circumstances. We can talk to Him at any and all times. He strengthens us through Word and Sacrament at worship services and through fellowship with other Christians. He refreshes us when we set aside private time to read and study His Word and to reflect privately with Him on our sins, His forgiving love, and a new direction and set of goals and purposes for our life.

▲ God's Love Makes a Difference

Begin this section commenting that God's love and forgiveness move us to stress the good in the attitudes and thoughts on which we choose to focus. Ask participants to work in small groups to complete the practice exercise, changing negative thoughts into positive ones. Then review responses as a whole group. Talk about the residual benefit for our children if we learn to approach situations with a positive attitude rooted and grounded in Christ's loving and guiding care.

▲ To Do at Home

Encourage participants to complete this activity privately

during the week ahead. Challenge participants to use the list as a guide for a plan of action rather than a series of items for personal reflection.

▲ Closing Prayer

Conclude the session, praying the prayer printed in the Study Guide or a prayer of your own.

Session 2

Meeting My Children's Needs

▲ Focus

Welcome everyone. Give each participant a copy of the Study Guide. Encourage participants to write their names on the front covers. Ask that they take the booklets home between sessions and bring them back each time the group meets.

▲ Objectives

That by the power of the Holy Spirit working through God's Word the participants will
1. affirm God's love for all children;
2. explain how the loving and forgiving power of God is evidenced in the lives of those who love and trust in Him;
3. explore how, responding to the love of God, we can meet the needs of children—specifically those in single-parent homes.

▲ Opening Prayer

Direct the attention of the group to the following words of Matthew 5:14–16, "You are the light of the world. A city on a hill cannot be hidden. Neither do people light a lamp and put it under a bowl. Instead they put it on its stand, and it gives light to everyone in the house. In the same way, let your light shine before men, that they may see your good deeds and praise your Father in heaven." Invite participants to join you in praying the prayer printed in the Study Guide.

▲ Focusing Our Attention

Ask participants to rank their favorite family activities and to share their rankings in pairs or small groups.

▲ The Love of a Parent

Read the introductory material. Reflect that because of sin, not every child is loved by his or her parent. Even the best of parents often fall short in their intentions and efforts toward their children. But God loves everyone with a pure and unchanging love. Invite participants to take notes on the evidence of God's love for children they find expressed in the verses included in this section. After about five minutes invite responses from the group to each item. Following are possible insights and comments.

1. The Maker of the entire universe creates each of us individually, uniquely, and specially.

2. In His love, God chose and planned for us to be adopted into His family through faith in Christ Jesus before the creation of the world.

3. Isaiah poetically describes God's love for us extending to our children as they also come to faith through the working of the Spirit. By God's blessing our children will also flourish in spiritual health like lush, green grass and hearty, well-watered trees.

4. These verses indicate Jesus' special love for children. He insisted parents be allowed to bring them to Him. "And He took the children in His arms, put His hands on them and blessed them." Note Jesus' individual, personal touch. In such a way He still touches lives through Baptism.

5. Through the witness of parents to their children, generation after generation will come to know and trust in God our Savior.

6. God desires to fill the missing places in our lives. He gives us families to love and care for and to be loved and cared for by them in return.

7. Saving knowledge of God and His love for us in Christ Jesus brings children peace.

▲ For the Children

Read introductory material aloud. Affirm God's presence and power in the lives of all who love and trust in Him. For those who are parenting alone, God is the guiding, directing, and encouraging invisible partner. Ask a volunteer to read the poem aloud as the rest of the group listens for evidence of God's influence in this parent's life. Continue with a discussion of the questions in this section. Possible answers follow.

1. The parent values the son as a work of art, a redeemed child of God, who possesses the genetic properties of both of his parents. The author addresses the poem to the absent parent and mentions telling the son about the good qualities of the absent parent he or she sees in the son. We don't know whether the missing parent is absent because of death or human choice. Regardless of the circumstances, the ability to focus on the good qualities of another is also a gift from God and may evidence the working of the Holy Spirit in the life of a believer.

2. The words, "Now he's God's—forgiven, free" elude to the son coming to faith.

3. Participants are likely to comment that they would expect to find a loving Christian atmosphere in this home. Continue with the next section.

▲ God's Power for Parenting

Introduce this portion of the lesson, emphasizing that as the Holy Spirit works in the believers' lives, they are motivated to love and care for others. Ask volunteers to read the scenarios in this section. Pausing after each to discuss it. Or put participants into groups and assign one or more scenarios and accompanying questions to each group. Then briefly review all the questions after assembling again as a whole group. Possible responses follow.

Meet Steve.

1. Most likely, the boys need to know that their father did indeed love and care about their mother. Being open about the difficulty of handling their mother's illness won't negate Steve's feelings for his wife. He needs to express his grief. The

boys may have concerns that they didn't "do" enough for their mother, that they resented her ill health, etc., which also needs to be discussed. They may also wonder whether their father would be similarly unaffected if they were to die.

2. Steve needs to assure his sons that he is sensitive to their feelings and to the different ways people grieve. His sons need to be assured that they will automatically be a part of any "new life" he makes for himself and that he will always love them.

3. Health-care providers are increasingly sensitive to the devastation that a long-term illness can have on a family. Support groups for children and spouses are available in many locations. The boys would have benefited from communicating their feelings in an ongoing and regular basis especially during their mother's illness.

4. Each member of the family might be put in touch with someone in the congregation or within the Christian community who has experienced a similar situation. Demonstrations of care and concern that include providing meals and assisting with household chores upon illness or the death of a family member are ways in which individual members can help. Encourage participants to think of specific ways to reach out to this family.

Meet Jeanne.

1. Encourage responses that illustrate the loving and forgiving attitude toward others that God manifests in the hearts of all of His children. Refer participants to the forgiving tone of the single parent in the poem "Our Son" read previously. It appears Jeanne needs to come to terms with her own feelings and express willingness to forgive. It has been said that it is impossible to hate someone for whom you are praying. Perhaps praying about her relationship with Kyle's father would be a good place for Jeanne to begin.

2. The Winter/Spring special edition of Newsweek (1990) reported that 42% of fathers fail to see their children after they divorce. For the children who were born out of wedlock, this figure is considerably higher. Because God is holy, He is not subject to the same frailties as human parents. He is, in fact, able to give us the unconditional and totally consistent and dependable love we will never find in any human relationship.

3. Affirm participant responses. If inappropriate attitudes and actions are noted, encourage taking steps to correct them.

Meet Darrell.

1. Affirm Darrell by pointing out all the "successes" he has had in raising his daughter. Perhaps a woman in the congregation might make herself available as a special older friend to Nicole and provide her on occasion with helpful female advice.

2. Nicole might be invited to assist with the church nursery, serve as a Sunday school teacher's helper, be involved in meals prepared at church, model in a fashion show, and other activities through which she might become acquainted with other Christian women.

▲ To Do at Home

Encourage participants—single and married parents alike—to do one or more of these activities during the coming week.

▲ Closing Prayer

Conclude the session praying the prayer printed in the Study Guide or invite a volunteer to lead the group praying extemporaneously.

Session 3

A New Day ... A New Start

▲ Focus

Welcome everyone. Give each participant a copy of the Study Guide. Encourage participants to write their names on the front covers. Ask that they take the booklets home between sessions and bring them back each time the group meets.

▲ Objectives

That by the power of the Holy Spirit working through the Word the participants will

1. recognize the negative effect guilt can bring to a person's life;

2. affirm the complete and total forgiveness Christ has won for us through His life, death, and resurrection;

3. express confident trust in Christ's ability to redirect, fortify, and encourage us as we seek to build a new life;

4. explore practical ways to leave the past behind as we work to build a brighter future.

▲ Opening Prayer

Lead the group in an extemporaneous prayer or pray the prayer printed in the Study Guide.

▲ Focusing Our Attention

Working as a large group, in small groups, or as partners, have participants explain how the type of vehicle they chose describes how they are feeling at the present time.

▲ That Old, Familiar Feeling

Read the introductory material aloud. Reflect briefly on the role of guilt in each of our lives. Invite participants to complete the items in this section individually. When everyone has finished, review responses.

1. Participants may share if they choose about some of the areas that cause them the most guilt. Force no one to share, however.

2. a. Mention that some scholars believe Psalm 38 in part describes an actual physical illness from which David suffered, although that illness is not specifically identified. Others believe that David was speaking metaphorically, using physical symptoms to describe how thoroughly guilt had overtaken him. Participants may be willing to share times in their lives when emotional burdens manifested themselves in physical symptoms.

b. Affirm the various responses identifying consequences of sin in our own lives and in the world around us.

3. David recognizes (verse 15) that God is the answer to his anguish. Note that he says definitively, "You will answer."

4. Emphasize that God desires the acknowledgment of sin and the weighty burden of its consequences in our lives to prepare our hearts for the forgiveness and salvation He offers us freely in Christ Jesus. Summaries of God's love will resemble the following.

verse 8—Compassion and grace are qualities of God; therefore He angers slowly and loves abundantly.

verse 9—He doesn't always accuse; neither does He remain angry forever.

verse 10—He doesn't give us what we deserve by virtue of our sinfulness.

verse 11—His love is as high as the heavens for those who fear Him.

verse 12—He has taken our sins away from us—as far away as east is from the west.

verse 13—His love for those who fear Him is like that of a loving father for his children.

verse 14—He knows our human condition with its weakness, limitations, and mortality.

verse 15—Our life passes quickly like grass and thrives but briefly as compared to a flower in a field.

verse 16—But soon we are gone and remembered no more, as though blown away by the wind.

verse 17—But God's love will remain forever with those who love and trust in Him.

5. Most likely participants marked the following verses.

a. Participants should have drawn an upward arrow beside verse 5 in which David describes Himself as a sinner from the time of his conception.

b. A downward arrow should be placed by verse 6 as it describes God's desire for truth in our inner parts (the center of our emotions and moral sensitivity).

c. In verses 7-12, which should be underlined, David explains his desire to be forgiven and made pure and happy.

d. Participants should have circled verse 13 in which David says he will teach transgressors the way of the Lord so that they may be converted.

▲ Removing the Blanket of Guilt

Read or ask a volunteer to read the introductory paragraph. Stress the all-consuming love of Jesus, which removes all guilt and frees us to be the people of God. Continue with a discussion of the questions, working through them as a whole group, or ask participants to work in small groups and briefly review each item later as a whole group.

1. For single parents, the whole issue of being single may be a source of guilt—whether they are divorced, never married, or feeling somehow responsible for the death of their spouse. While being single (and a parent) is much more acceptable today than it was even a generation ago, there is still a persistent attitude in society that "married is better." Ask participants to react with their experiences to that idea. The Study Guide asks, "How valid are these feelings?" Point out that feelings are always difficult to change and are always valid to the person expressing them. Yet how often don't we say, "Oh, you shouldn't feel that way."

Affirm that sometimes all of us feel guilt legitimately because of the wrong things we have done and the hurt and harm that have resulted. Christ's forgiveness is complete. Forgiven by Him, we must also allow His power to enable us to forgive ourselves.

2. Point out that there are two kinds of guilt: specific and nonspecific. Specific guilt occurs over some behavior of which we are fully aware. Nonspecific guilt is that feeling of "I must have done something wrong, but I don't know what I did." This is the type of guilt Satan most likes to perpetuate because it's so difficult to eradicate totally.

The psalmist confesses before God both the sins he knows and acknowledges as evidence of his rebellion against God and also those sins, which because of his sinfulness, he is unaware of having committed. God's forgiveness for us in Christ cleanses us from all sin.

3. Answers may vary. Comment that we sometimes refuse to let go of our sins because we may wish for them to retain their hold on us or we think they are too great for God to forgive. Also, realistically, while our sins may be forgiven, we still often have to bear the consequences of that sin.

4. God invites us to confess our sins in order to receive the complete forgiveness He freely offers through Christ.

5. a. God forgets every sin He has forgiven in Christ Jesus.

b. We can give our unsettled hearts over to God trusting that He will carry all our burdens—including those that cause us to feel unforgiven.

▲ Forgiven, Restored, Ready to Begin Again

Read the introductory paragraph. Encourage participants to consider these practical suggestions, based on Philippians 3:13–14, for leaving the past behind and moving on with life as God's new people. Suggest they take a minute or two to read and reflect upon these verses privately. Then invite comments and insights before asking participants to work in small groups as they continue with this section. Briefly review each numbered item as a whole group after the small-group discussion. The following insights may be helpful.

1. Point out the importance of single parents talking to their children about how they feel. Carmen might find that if she explained to her children her need to "prove herself," they might be able to reassure her, build her confidence, and help her work out a plan for attending the activities that are most important to them.

2. Throughout this lesson, and again in the following lessons, discuss and encourage participants to share the experiences they have had with professional counseling, particularly as it relates to single-parent issues. Many Christians who have been helped greatly by professional intervention are hesitant to mention their experiences because they believe that Christians shouldn't need to seek help outside the church or God's Word. This concept undermines the talents and gifts God has given to Christian counselors whom God has chosen just for this role. If you are unable to suggest names of Christian counselors in your area, make certain that this information is available through your pastor or church staff.

Affirm that the time comes to leave the past behind and trust God's help in building a future. The most important item to leave in the past is guilt over failures. Holding on to sins that Christ has paid the ultimate price to forgive merely guarantees bringing the hurts and pain of the past into the future.

3. Charlene feels guilt as her relationship with Walter develops. Charlene may deal with her feelings in a positive way by turning the situation over to God, asking for His direction and guidance, and maintaining opening communication with all those involved.

▲ To Do at Home

Encourage participants to put into practice one or more of the applications from the "Forgiven, Restored, and Ready to Begin Again" section during the coming week.

▲ Closing Prayer

Lead the group in the responsive reading. Then offer a prayer in which you thank God for the comfort He promises to bring to all who love and trust in Him.

Session 4

The Single Parent and the Church

▲ Focus

Welcome everyone. Give each participant a copy of the Study Guide. Encourage participants to write their names on the front covers. Ask that they take the booklets home between sessions and bring them back for the final session.

▲ Objectives

That by the power of the Holy Spirit working through the word the participants will

1. identify the church as the body of Christ, concerned with sharing the love of Jesus to persons both inside and outside the church;

2. recognize the qualities God desires to bring to all who are members of His church;

3. acknowledge Christ's forgiveness for the times we fail to live as the people of God;

4. identify ways we may more effectively reach out to others with the love of Jesus.

▲ Opening Prayer

Lead or ask a volunteer to lead the group in prayer, praying extemporaneously or praying the prayer printed in the Study Guide.

▲ Focusing Our Attention

Ask participants to work in small groups to share their choice of the body part that best describes them.

▲ God's Church—The Body of Christ

Ask participants for words or phrases that they feel describe the "perfect church." If possible, list these on a chalkboard for reference throughout the lesson.

Invite volunteers to each read one of the paragraphs in this section. Underscore the blessings God brings to His people through the fellowship of believers—the church. Continue with a discussion of the questions, inviting participants to work in small groups if you choose.

1. Paul identifies the following characteristics: compassion, kindness, humility, gentleness and patience, forgiveness, love, unity, peace, thankfulness, the indwelling of the Word of Christ, teaching and admonishing with all wisdom, singing of psalms, hymns, and spiritual songs with gratitude to God, doing all in the name of the Lord Jesus Christ. Compare the attributes Paul lists with the suggestions made by the class.

2. Urge the class to think of as many examples as possible.

3. Invite participants to share openingly about how well their congregation meets the needs of single parents as well as provide them with opportunities to serve.

4. Ask participants to define family. Ask, **Is a single person living alone a family? Does there need to be more than one generation represented in a household in order for it to be considered a family? If the church is too "family-oriented," is it focusing too heavily on the traditional dad-mom-two kids-and-a-dog definition part of the problem?**

Comment that according to Ephesians 2:19–22, members of the church are fellow citizens (with no designation of family status), equal in status because of their bond to Christ. Together—as a family unit—members of a congregation are a dwelling for the Holy Spirit.

5. Although God has called His faithful followers to take a stand against sin and sinful lifestyles among those both inside and outside the church, malice and slander have no place in the church. God desires for us be kind and compassionate to one another, to forgive one another because God through Christ has forgiven us, and to live a life of love as imitators of Christ.

▲ Communicating Our Needs to Each Other

Read or invite volunteer to read the information in this section aloud to the group. Then ask participants to discuss the numbered items in pairs or small groups before reassembling and sharing briefly the highlights of the discussion of each item. In order to allow more time for whole-group response and sharing, either assign each group one item to discuss before reassembling for the whole-group discussion or discuss each item as a whole group.

As participants reflect upon the experiences of single parents, encourage them to dwell on how communication broke down rather than fixing blame for the hurt feelings. If the class is comfortable doing so, have individual members role-play the thoughts expressed and perhaps add thoughts of their own. Encourage participants to analyze how similar situations might develop in their own congregations and discuss specific steps to prevent that from happening. Possible responses to the questions follow.

1. a. Perhaps congregational members thought that by taking an interest in Melanie they might be perceived as trying to find out information about Melanie to spread to others or, on the other hand, of accepting and/or promoting having children outside of marriage. Perhaps after Joey's birth it was easier to focus on the baby rather than on the circumstances relating to his birth.

b. Answers will vary. Stress the importance of showing love and concern for all others in a spirit reminiscent of the fact that we all sin and daily require forgiveness for the things we have done. Simply ignoring young women and young men whose children are born outside of marriage is not helpful.

2. a. Cal recognized his need for the strength God offers through the Word and the Sacrament of the Lord's Supper. He also needed the support and encouragement of worshiping together with other believers.

b. From Cal's comments we may conclude that those wishing to support him need to be especially understanding of what may be interpreted as coolness or lack of interest in their friendship. Patience and understanding will be especially helpful in relating to him. Perhaps someone who has had a similar experience might be most successful in helping Cal through this rough time.

3. a. Perhaps Miranda's friends simply didn't know what to say to help her and feared saying something that might make her feel worse. Emphasize the importance of taking the initiative to help those who are going through a difficult time.

b. Miranda's experience will provide her with the understanding that will prove helpful when she has the opportunity to offer support and encouragement to someone in a similar situation.

4. a. People cannot be expected to meet the needs of others if they are consciously kept in ignorance about those needs. Emphasize the importance of open and constructive communication.

b. Ruth continued to meet together with her fellow believers to receive the benefits God provides through Word and Sacrament.

5. a. Affirm participant responses. If no one mentions it, suggest Damon take the initiate and invite others to do things with him or to involve himself in programs and activities so that he might continue to benefit from the friendship and concern of others.

b. Damon's words elude to the importance of providing support and care for those who have lost love ones long past the time of the funeral.

▲ Reaffirming God's Challenge

Read the introductory material and Philippians 2:1–4 aloud.

1. God desires us to possess and demonstrate His love; to be one in the Spirit and in purpose; not be ambitious for personal gain; in humility to consider others better than ourselves; and to be concerned for the interests of others.

2–3. Encourage group suggestions. Make sure a list is compiled and that someone has responsibility for seeing that these suggestions are considered by the groups or individuals responsible for implementation. Work to turn group suggestions into a reality for the benefit of the life and health of your congregation.

▲ To Do at Home

Encourage participants to do this activity during the week ahead.

▲ Closing Prayer

Divide the group into two groups to pray the closing litany or appoint one person as leader while the group prays the response.

Session 5

Forward with Jesus

▲ Focus

Welcome everyone to the final session of this course. Make sure each participant has a copy of the Study Guide. Briefly review the topics covered in the preceding four sessions. Comment that today's session will wrap things up with a forward-looking emphasis on a Christ-powered new beginning.

▲ Objectives

That by the power of the Holy Spirit working through God's Word the participants will
1. describe the stages of grief and identify which, if any, stage they are in;

2. affirm that God in Christ empowers us to accept that which has occurred in our lives and enables us to refocus our lives in service to Him;

3. express joy in knowing that God in Christ loves them and cares for them at all times and in all situations.

▲ Opening Prayer

Lead or ask a volunteer to lead the group in prayer, praying extemporaneously or praying the prayer printed in the Study Guide.

▲ Focusing Our Attention

Ask participants to work in pairs or in groups of three or four to explain their choice of the song title that best describes a recent event or mood in their family.

▲ Breaking Through—with God's Help

Read the introductory paragraphs in this section aloud to the group. Continue with the discussion of the items in this section as a whole group.

1. Answers will vary. Encourage sharing by beginning with an example from your experience.

2. Isaiah 42:16 is most emphatic—it leaves no doubt that God intends to do what He says. He promises to lead, guide, turn darkness into light, and make rough places smooth. He then adds emphasis by saying again that He will do these things. He adds further emphasis by saying that He will not forsake us.

▲ From Grief to Acceptance

Ask a succession of volunteers to read the information in this section—including the five stages of grief—aloud to the group, paragraph by paragraph. Clarify, discuss, and allow participants to share about the grieving process. Invite participants to work through the items in this section individually. Then reassemble everyone and invite comments and insights.

1. Encourage participants to share only if they are comfortable doing so.

2. Summarize these verses as follows: God has created us, formed us, redeemed us, and called us by name; we are His, and He will always remain with us to help and protect us.

3. As a result of our suffering we may ultimately be better able to understand, relate to, and help someone who experiences what we have experienced.

▲ From "I Can't" to "I Can"

Read the introductory material aloud to the group. Stress that trusting Jesus as Savior and living for Him is more than mere positive thinking—the benefits of His power and presence transcend any results that could occur from simply possessing a positive outlook. Continue to discuss the numbered items with the whole group. Possible responses follow.

1. Reminding oneself of these words will help to emphasize the role Christ has and desires to play with ever increasing influence in the lives of those who belong to Him.

2. Paul knows that only by relying on Christ and God's grace can he do anything. God gives strength to those who find their strength in Him.

3. Ask a volunteer to read this section from Ephesians aloud. Invite participants to share with the group.

▲ The Need for Help

Proceed as previously with this section. If possible, be prepared with names, locations, and telephone numbers of Christian counselors in your area. Your pastor or church staff may have suggestions.

1. Emphasize the importance for those desiring to follow God's will in their lives to receive the advice and encouragement of professionals whose approach is Bible-based and Christ-centered.

2. If we have asked God to speak to us through the counseling of a trusted professional or friend, we should trust that God will speak through that person.

▲ Dating and a New Beginning

Read or invite a volunteer to read the beginning information in this section aloud. Then continue with a whole-group discussion of the numbered items. It may be tempting for the class to become diverted by personal issues during this discussion. Don't allow participants to get so far afield in their discussion that the lesson loses its focus. Consider the following during your discussion.

1. The world may not always tell us what is best for us. As our minds are transformed from worldly values to serving God, God's will becomes clearer to us.

2. God often speaks His Word to us through other Christians as we worship and talk with them. The influences we allow in our lives contribute a great deal to what we hear, where we look for answers, and ultimately to what we come to believe.

▲ From Grief to Joy

Continue as in the previous two sections, reading and discussing as a whole group. Contrast joy with a sense of acceptance and inner peace. Both may be evidenced in the lives of those who have recovered from grief.

1. Before His suffering and death, Jesus promised His disciples that even though their grief would be intense, they would once again experience great joy.

2. The resurrection of Jesus is a joy given to every Christian that cannot be diminished by circumstances of this world. Allow participants to share some of the items they have listed if they feel comfortable doing so.

Conclude the study on an upbeat note, focusing on the joys God has promised to us both here on earth and in heaven.

If this class is made up primarily of single parents, the group may have become so comfortable that they may wish to continue meeting as a social/support/study group to explore additional material related to single parenting or other topics. Encourage the group to pursue this goal, and if possible, provide them with resources and/or personnel to make this happen.

▲ To Do at Home

Encourage participants to do this activity during the week ahead.

▲ Closing Prayer

Lead the group, praying either the prayer printed in the Study Guide or another of your own.

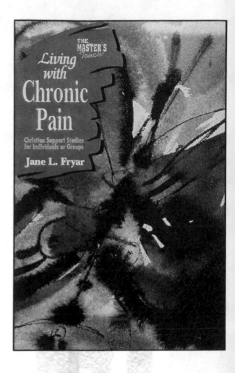